HAMMOND PUBLIC LIBRARY

3 1161 00062 9348

S0-BSO-926

— '68 1 0 7 5 2   y791.5

O.P.   Food stains

	DATE DUE	
MAY 27 '71 Hansen		
AUG 1 7 '76 HP		

Lewis, Shari
   Making easy puppets.

WITHDRAWN

MAIN CHILDREN'S ROOM

Hammond Public Library
Hammond, Ind.

MAKING EASY
PUPPETS

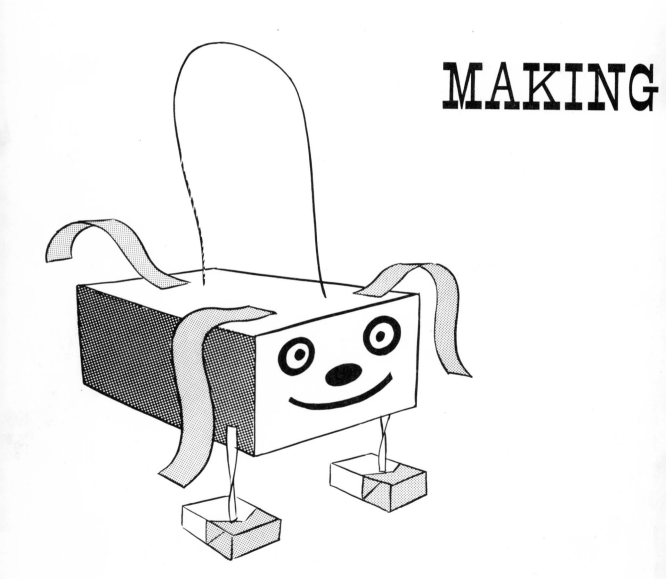

MAKING

EASY

PUPPETS

by Shari Lewis

illustrated by Larry Lurin

E. P. Dutton & Co., Inc.   New York

Hammond Public Library
Hammond, Ind.

'68 | 0 7 5 2
391

Also by Shari Lewis
Folding Paper Masks (with Lillian Oppenheimer)
Folding Paper Puppets (with Lillian Oppenheimer)
Folding Paper Toys (with Lillian Oppenheimer)
Dear Shari
Fun with the Kids
Knowing and Naming (with Jacquelyn Reinach)
Thinking and Imagining (with Jacquelyn Reinach)
Looking and Listening (with Jacquelyn Reinach)

Copyright, © 1958, 1960, 1967 by Shari Lewis.
All rights reserved. Printed in the U.S.A.
No part of this book may be reproduced in any form without permission
in writing from the publisher, except by a reviewer who wishes to quote
brief passages in connection with a review written for inclusion in a
magazine, newspaper or broadcast. Published simultaneously in Canada
by Clarke, Irwin & Company Limited, Toronto and Vancouver.
Library of Congress Catalog Card Number: 67-20128
First edition.

main

y 791.5

Contents

Puppets for Play

(Puppet toys that are just for fun)

Puppet Bodies

Puppet Stages

Puppets and Things to Do with Them

Puppets and Very Small People

Puppet Aids for the Teacher and Group Leader, and a Holiday Index

Puppet Books — A Bibliography

Puppets Past

(A Short Study of the Long History of Puppets)

Most experts agree that puppetry started in China, but when or how isn't absolutely certain. According to one story, Wu-Ti, the emperor of an ancient Chinese dynasty, was overcome with grief at the death of his favorite wife. He ordered the court magician to summon back her spirit, and by dint of a darkened room and a distant screen, the magician was able to create the shadow of a moving figure vaguely resembling the wife, which apparently satisfied the emperor.

Although I wouldn't bet a penny on the truth of that tale, the Chinese shadow puppet show is generally regarded as the oldest form of puppetry, so let me tell you a bit about shadow puppets in general, and Chinese shadow puppets in particular.

A shadow puppet is a cutout figure, generally translucent and beautifully colored. It is placed close to a screen, and the light from a lamp placed behind the puppet passes through the translucent skin of the cutout figure onto the screen. The audience, sitting on the other side of the screen, can see the colors and the outline of the puppet. Generally, shadow puppets are moved by three rods: the main rod, from which the puppet is suspended, is attached to its neck, while the other two rods are joined to its wrists. The puppeteer usually holds the main rod in one hand and manipulates the other two rods with the other hand.

Chinese shadow puppets are often made of donkey skin, and are incredibly tough and durable in spite of their fragile appearance. The dried skins of sheep, water buffaloes, pigs, and even certain kinds of fish are also used.

Other ancient peoples made shadow puppets, too. Around A.D. 1000 they were certainly in existence in Java. There are two theories as to the origin of the Javanese performances: one is that they started as ancestor worship (the shadowy figures symbolizing the spirits of the dead); while the other thought is that these figures and plays were shown during initiation rites, to teach the young men the history and legends of their race. Whatever the original purpose of the shadow puppet (or "Wayang Purwa") performance, it was primarily the puppet that counted, and not its shadow. The audience was divided by the screen, with the men sitting on the same side as the puppeteer, watching the puppets being moved by him, and the women sitting on the other side of the screen, viewing only the shadow.

This separation of men and women at puppet shows existed in many countries. In China it is explained by a legend concerning a puppetmaster named Yang Shih, who was said to have made the first puppets and performed with them at the court of the Chu emperor, Mu Wang, in the tenth century B.C. They say that on one occasion the emperor felt that the puppets were winking at his wives, and he ordered the puppeteer put to death. But before the executioner could approach Yang Shih, he quickly cut his puppets apart to prove that they weren't really alive. The emperor allowed Yang Shih to continue performing, but just to make sure that there would be no further flirtation, he forbade his wives to watch any such performance, except from behind a screen.

All of the ancient Oriental and Middle Eastern peoples had

shadow puppets, but the figures differed from country to country. In Siam, they were even more elaborately carved than in Java, but they did not have as many moving parts. They were more like outlines of statues — sort of decorative pictures of the characters they portrayed.

The Turks and the Greeks developed a new method for operating shadow figures. The innovation was that the rods, which in the Siamese, Javanese, and Chinese puppets came up from below the figure, now were worked from the sides (that is, horizontally) as well. This gave the puppeteer much more control. The Turkish puppets also differed in that they had a loose joint at the waist so that the characters could easily bend forward to make sweeping bows to the ground, or lean backward to gaze up at the sky. The whole effect was very lively and quite slapstick. The shadow puppet shows in Turkey, instead of revolving around religious or historical stories, were often about a character called Karagoz, which means Black Eye, and the traditional Turkish puppet had a big eye, heavily outlined in black, with a black pupil, which gave it a kind of Byzantine, almost Egyptian appearance. The Greek puppet figure was also called Karagoz, and he was always hungry. His hunger was immense — that was his theme song — and he would constantly say that he had fasted so long he couldn't live any longer, and while waiting in the kitchen of a house, he would eat the dishes, the dishcloth, a bucket of soap which he thought was cream cheese, and so on.

Soon after the development of the shadow (or flat) rod puppet, the three-dimensional rod puppet was born. He didn't hide behind a screen, and was beautifully carved and dressed according to the customs and myths of the country. He was usually used to tell the same stories and to portray the same traditional characters that had been enacted by the shadow puppets. Rod puppets of this kind, and jointed dolls, have even been uncovered in many ancient Egyptian tombs.

The very oldest story of the invention of rod puppets seems to be the one recorded in China, in the Tang epoch. A Khan, who was the leader of a nomadic tribe, had surrounded a city. Knowing that the Khan's wife was very temperamental, the minister of the surrounded city commanded that a puppet be made in the form of a beautiful girl, and with the assistance of some contraption or other — probably rods — made this girl puppet dance on top of the city walls. The Khan's wife, seeing the dancing girl, became very upset because she thought that, if the Khan captured the city, he would take this dancing beauty to be one of his wives, and she (the Khan's present wife) would lose the Khan's love and good will. The danger seemed to her so great and so real that the terrified wife persuaded her husband to abandon his siege of the city.

Strings instead of rods were attached to these jointed figures during the late Egyptian dynasties, and stringed puppets got their proper name, Marionettes, in Europe during the third or fourth century A.D. Puppeteers used to travel from town to town, performing the story of the Nativity on small stages built on the back of covered wagons. The stringed figure of the puppet who portrayed Mary was called a "little Mary" or Marionette, and that is the term used today to refer to all puppets operated by strings.

Hand puppets (or "bag" puppets, as they are sometimes called, because their bodies are made of a bag covering the hand) seem to have evolved first in China, too, but hand puppets the world over have been based on the same traditional characters. They are rowdy, and the classic man puppet has a long nose, a mouth that stretches from ear to ear, a hump on his back (sometimes two), a buffoon's hat with a tassel, he carries a stick, and it really doesn't matter whether this hand puppet is called Petroushka (in Russia), Polichinelle (in France), Punch (in England), Hanswurst (in Germany), Punchinello (in Italy), Casparek (in Czechoslovakia), or Karagoz (in Turkey and Greece), because they are all members of the same family! They even speak in the same strange voice. The puppeteer produces a very peculiar sound by putting a kind of small whistle in his mouth (my father always called this whistle a schwazzle), and the Punch and Judy voice is created by pressing the whistle to the roof of the mouth with the back of the tongue and speaking through it. (There's a narrow opening in the schwazzle.) The voice in the English Punch says, "Hey, Judy, Judy, Judy! Throw down the baby, Judy!" The voice is loud and shrill, and the words are not always understandable, but very distinctive, and always repeated a great deal.

The classic Chinese hand puppets sound and look very much like the European ones. However, the Chinese hand puppets were often used to tell historical legends, while generally the type of material performed by the European hand puppets was simply comic. Today Chinese puppet shows are being utilized to spread political and social information. This has also proved quite effective in the tiny towns and farm villages in India, where health habits and modern methods of agriculture are being taught by traveling government puppet troupes.

In Europe, shadow puppets became quite fashionable after the French Revolution. One wonderful innovation that the French made was adding strings (as well as the rods) and weights to the shadow figures so that a limb, held up by the string, would drop of its own volition because of the weights. Another bit of progress occurred at the turn of the century when the electric light was substituted for the flames that had previously been used to create the shadows.

Before the invention of radio and television, puppetry was a very popular form of home entertainment. Many eighteenth- and nineteenth-century books contained instructions on how to make easy hand and stringed figures. People made hand shadows for one another by twisting their hands and fingers into amusing shapes, then placing their hands in front of a bright light in an otherwise darkened room. In this way, distinct shadows would be cast upon a wall. Puppets were even created that were moved by magnets, but it wasn't until the twentieth century that puppets became truly mechanized. TV and motion pictures have produced figures that are manipulated electronically and by remote control. They are astounding and quite lifelike, but, in my opinion, lack the spontaneity, charm, warmth, and humanity that can be found only when the puppeteer is in direct contact with his alter ego.

Perhaps this is the pleasure that puppetry offers us today — the fact that, in this wonderful world of marvelous machines, we can definitely do one thing better than the best machine — we can give life and love to a tiny puppet, and give pleasure to ourselves and others as we do so.

Jack B. Nimble

With the drop of a handkerchief, you can produce a puppet show-man who is a show in himself. Jack B. Nimble can skate, dance, walk, sit, hop, or jump over a candlestick.

You will need:
>A large man's handkerchief
>A pencil
>Nail polish (optional)

Here's How: Spread the handkerchief on a flat surface and fold the top corner down to meet the bottom corner. Make a knot right at that bottom point (A), then open the triangle once again. Tie a knot (a tiny one this time) in the corner of the handkerchief that is to your right (B). Place the back of your right wrist over the first knot you tied, and, with your left hand, pull down the bit

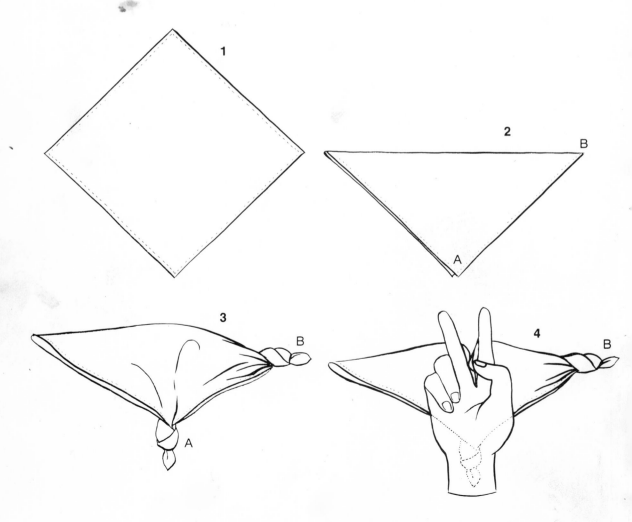

of the fabric that you will see peeking through your right pointer and middle fingers. With your right thumb, press this piece of cloth firmly into your right palm. Now fold down the pinkie and ring fingers of your right hand.

Grasp the unknotted corner of the handkerchief (which is to your left) with your left hand, and wrap it over the two folded fingers, and tuck it securely under the tips of these fingers. Tuck the knot (which is to your right) and any excess fabric into the bottom of the cloth at the wrist. This will keep Jack B. Nimble from falling apart during his performance.

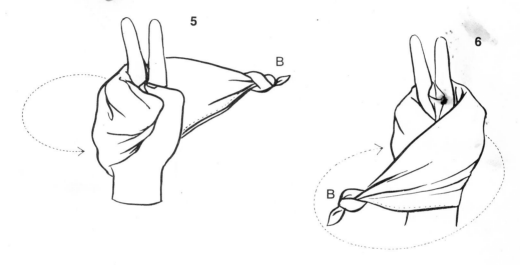

Turn your hand around and stand Jack on his twinkly toes (which are, of course, your finger tips) and, as you move your fingers, watch him walk away with the show. You can pencil in features on his face (which is the big knot), and if you want to give him shoes, color your nails with bright nail polish.

The Funny Bunny

Here's a rabbit you can pull out of your pocket anytime.

You will need:
> A handkerchief
> A rubber band

Here's How: Hold the handkerchief by two adjacent corners as in the first picture. Place both corners in the same hand and grab the handkerchief (next picture) with the two corners sticking above your fist. Now bring the bottom end of the handkerchief around the two ends, keeping them together as you make a knot in the very same spot where you were holding the handkerchief.

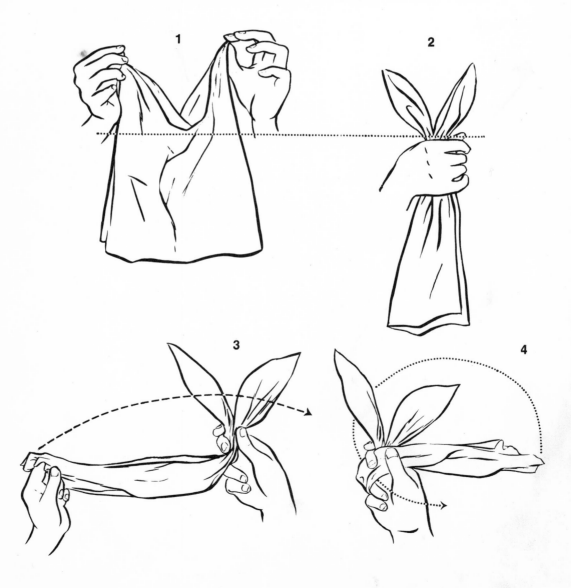

You now have a knot forming the Bunny's face, and two ends sticking up above it, becoming his ears. Shove your pointer finger deep into the knot (*behind* the face) and drape the rest of the handkerchief around your thumb and middle finger, which are extended in opposite directions. To complete the body, see page 65 for instructions on the drape body. Your pointer finger inside the knot will move the head, your thumb and middle finger will become hands.

Boo Hoo, the Little Ghost

You haven't a ghost of a chance of scaring anyone with this little puppet, but he will make a spirited friend!

You will need:
>A handkerchief
>A crayon
>A rubber band

Here's How: Knot one corner of the handkerchief and draw a face on the knot. Stick your pointer finger into the knot (behind the face) and drape the rest of the handkerchief around your outstretched thumb and middle finger. Hook a rubber band right around the thumb, across the back of your hand and around your middle finger, to complete the puppet body. Your pointer finger now controls his head, and the other two fingers become his arms. See if you can make him scratch his head. He can applaud, bow, and rub his tummy, too! Why not let this enchanting ghost be the host of your next Halloween party?

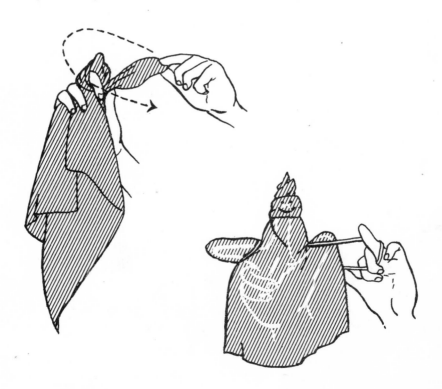

Sad Sack, the Bunny

The solution to your "what-to-do-on-a-rainy-day" problem is in the bag.

You will need:

      A brown paper shopping bag (the smallest you can find in the house)
      Scissors
      Crayons

Here's How: Draw a colorful bunny on a closed brown paper bag so that the mouth is half on the bottom flap and half on the bag itself (see picture 1). The top of his head should meet the fold at the top of the bag. Now turn the bag around and on the back of the bag draw the ears, so that they connect at the fold with the top of the bunny's head. Cut out the ears along the outline, except where they are joined (at the fold) to the top of the head.

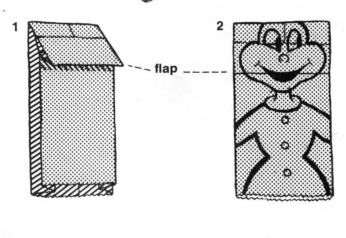

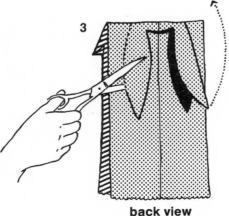

back view

Stand the ears up straight and your bunny is complete, but speechless. Only *you* can make him talk. Place your hand into the bag so that your fingers go inside the flap. By opening and closing your hand, you can make him open and close his mouth. Next rainy day, the only sad sack around your house will be Sad Sack, the paper bag bunny.

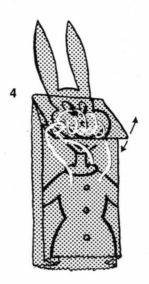

Jack-in-the-Bag Marionette

This bunny puppet will dance to beat the band (and that band can consist of thirty-six union musicians on your TV set, or one humming child).

You will need:
- A paper bag
- Crayon
- Scissors
- String
- Long pencil or ruler

Here's How: Hold the bag upside down with the open part toward the floor. Draw a face near the fold at the top of the bag. Decide where the neck is going to be, and cut the entire area of the bag below the neck into thin strips. Fluff out the "face" part of the bag and tie a string around the neck, good and tight. Pull out a few strands on each side for arms (cut to arm length). Leave an extra length of string attached to each wrist, so you can make your Jack-in-the-Bag bound about! Tie a string at the waist. Separate the strips below the waist into two equal bundles and tie near the bottom for legs.

Make two tiny holes at the top of the head and thread a good length of string through the holes. Attach this string to the center of a long pencil or ruler. Tie one of the "arm" strings to each end of the pencil or ruler, and you've made basic marionette controls.

Captain Cod

You can fish a puppet out of a paper bag.

You will need:
>A small paper bag
>A rubber band
>Scissors

Here's How: Put your right hand all the way into a paper bag. Your fingers are going to form the top of your fish's mouth, and your thumb will be the bottom lip. With your left hand, press the paper at the bottom of the bag down into the furrow between your thumb and the other fingers. Now, as you move your thumb up and down, the fish will open and close his mouth. Poke holes for eyes, or cut U-shaped openings, and fold up the tiny flaps for eyelashes. Slip a rubber band around your wrist (a piece of string tied around your wrist will do, too). Fluff out the edge of the paper bag to form the funny, finny, fancy tail fin, and your fish is finished!!

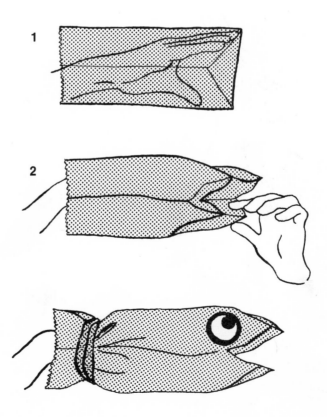

Captain Carrot

If you carrot all for puppets, you'll love this little carrot pirate.

You will need:

     A fat carrot
     An old sock
     Three paper reinforcements or paper stars
     One thumbtack
     A toothpick
     Scissors
     A handkerchief
     A rubber band

Here's How: Cut off the toe of the sock for his hat. Just turn up a tiny brim and place it jauntily on top of the carrot. Cut another sliver of sock for his mustache. Stick the thumbtack through the

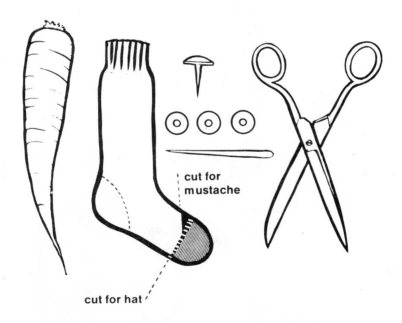

cut for
mustache

cut for hat

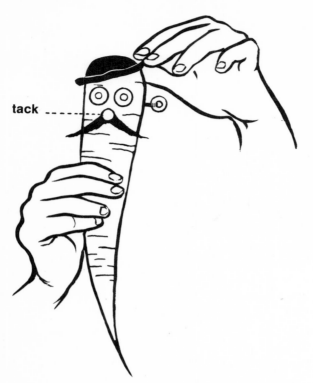

tack

widest spot in the center of the mustache and right into the carrot. (The thumbtack will become his nose.) Wet two paper reinforcements and attach them in the appropriate spots for eyes. Break off a tiny piece of toothpick and stick it into the carrot about where his ear should be, and paste the third paper reinforcement onto the toothpick as a dangling pirate's earring. You can change his face if you wish by using paper stars for eyes.

Using the rest of the carrot as your "stick," make the body (see page 66 for easy instructions).

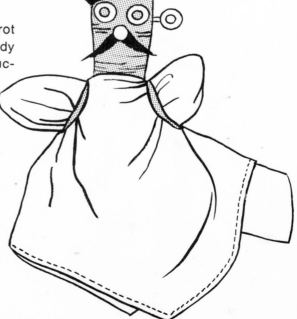

Ella Fant, the Pachyderm Puppet

Ask Mother to help you make this cute vegetable puppet. The next time she goes shopping ask her please to pick out two small turnips shaped like elephant's heads, that is, shaped like round balls with long curved noses.

You will need:

        Two turnips (Squashes would do, too)
        A knife
        Two or three thumbtacks
        Two toothpicks
        One other toothpick, broken in half
        Jingle bell (optional)

Here's How: When you have these things assembled on the kitchen table, ask Mother to cut two ears (see diagram) from one of the turnips. (One ear cut from each side of the same turnip.) Now the rest of that turnip can be used for cooking. The other turnip will become the elephant. Have a deep V-shaped slice cut into the turnip at the base of the long curved part (which, of course, will be the trunk). This V-shaped slice is the mouth.

At the base of the vegetable (see picture for exact spot), cut a deep hole, wide enough for your pointer finger to slide right into.

1

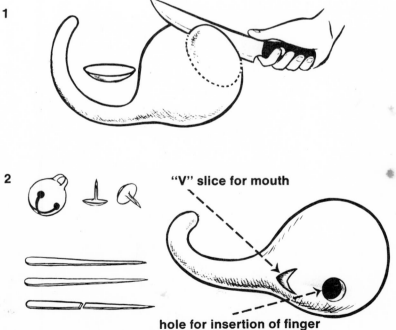

2

"V" slice for mouth

hole for insertion of finger

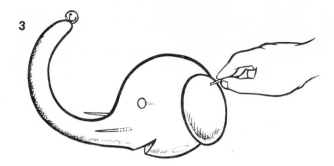

3

With the broken pieces of toothpick, fasten the large round ears onto the side of Ella Fant's head. Push in the two thumbtacks as eyes, and two whole toothpicks make perfect tusks on the sides of the trunk. For the finishing touch, you might fasten a jingle bell to the top of the trunk with another toothpick. Now make a drape body (see page 65 for easy instructions) and when completed, insert your pointer finger into the hole in the bottom of the turnip. Lo and behold, a turnip elephant will turn up on the end of your finger.

Now that you've got an elephant on your hands, why not let him star in your next puppet play? A circus show would be nice, or how about the story of Noah's Ark? You needn't worry about remembering his lines. They say an elephant never forgets!

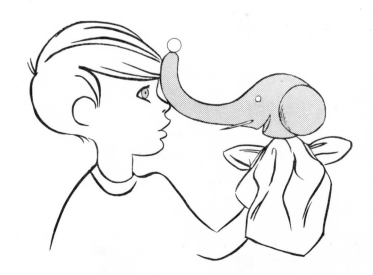

Apple Jack 'n' Jill

This cute fruit puppet will be the apple of your eye.

You will need:
        One round bright-red apple
        A needle
        A teaspoon
        A handkerchief
        A rubber band

Here's How: Sketch big pumpkin-like features on the apple, using the point of the needle to break the skin as you draw. With a teaspoon, carefully scoop out the features that you have outlined. The white pulp of the apple will then show through the eyes, nose, and mouth. This will shine brightly against the red skin of the apple face.

Have Mother core the apple by cutting a hole that extends halfway up the center of the apple. Place a large handkerchief over your pointer finger and place your finger into the apple-core hole. After you have done this, put a rubber band around your outstretched thumb, extend it around the back of your hand, and hook it around your middle finger. These two fingers will then become your Apple Jack's hands.

Your apple man can also serve as a candleholder if, instead of coring the apple, you dig a tiny hole in the top of the apple and insert a little birthday candle well into his head.

Either way, doesn't he look good enough to eat?

Willie B. Brave, the Matchbox Indian

This matchbox Indian puppet, complete with headdress, will be a real feather in your cap.

You will need:

> A small, empty, wooden matchbox
> A handkerchief
> A tiny feather
> Construction paper and paste, or colored plastic tape
>   (You need two colors, one light and one dark)
> Scissors
> A rubber band
> Pipe cleaner

Here's How: Separate the two parts of the empty wooden matchbox, and throw away the inside drawer. Cover the outer shell of the box with light-colored (or red) construction paper or plastic tape. Cut a thin band of dark paper or tape and attach a tiny feather to it. (If you don't have a real one, a paper feather will do.) Paste this headdress near the open top of the matchbox.

Now cut and paste dark eyes, a big nose, a snarly mouth, and two huge ears to the covered matchbox. Use the drape body (see page 65) for this puppet. The final touch is a pipe cleaner hatchet (paste on a tiny paper blade).

Milk Carton Creature

Here's a creature who will know (and be able to recite) all the poems and jokes that every child in the house knows. Amazing isn't it?

You will need:

        1 milk carton
        Pencil
        Scissors
        Paints, brushes, and 1 teaspoonful soap flakes or deter-
            gent; or construction paper and rubber cement; or
            colored plastic tape
        1 knitted sock

Here's How: Stand a milk carton upright and draw a pencil line all around the middle of the container. Along this line, cut the front and two sides of the container. Do *not* cut the back. You now have two halves, connected only in back. Open the two halves until they meet in back, folding the solid back strip of the carton in half. The edges of the top and the bottom of the carton are now touching each other. On the other side of the container, you will find two separate pockets. Put your thumb in the bottom pocket, and your other fingers in the top pocket. As you open and close your hand, the top and bottom separate and come together again. If you draw eyes, nose, and top lip on the top — lower lip and chin on the bottom — you'll have a talking puppet. The features can be painted. Put the soap flakes in the paint, or wipe the brush over a cake of soap before you dip it in the paint. This will make the paint stick to the waxy surface. The features can also be cut out of construction paper and fastened on with rubber cement, or cut out of colored plastic tape and pressed on. I cut the foot off a knitted sock and used the ankle band to cover my arm at the point where it entered the back of the puppet.

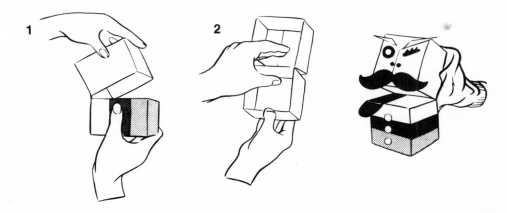

Smokey the Santa

Here's a Santa puppet who will stand on his head to become a candy container for your Christmas party!

You will need:

        A flip-top cigarette box
        White crepe or construction paper
        Glue or rubber cement
        Scissors
        Red crepe paper
        Red thread
        Cotton
        2 gummed stars
        1 Christmas seal or a small circle of red paper
        Pencil

Here's How: Cover the entire cigarette box with white paper, but make sure that the flip-top lid can still open and close. Stand the box upright on a table, with the flip-top opening on the bottom, facing you. To make Santa's hat, cut a strip of red crepe paper (approximately five by ten inches). Apply a band of rubber cement along the edge of one of the ten-inch sides of the paper. Then wrap this sticky edge of the paper around what is now the very top of the box. Most of the crepe paper will be standing up *above* the box. Carefully gather the top of the crepe paper together and, with a small piece of red thread, tie the paper in this position so that the hat comes to a point. Now cover the point of the hat with a ball of cotton. Next, conceal the spot where the hat is attached to the box with a band of cotton, rubber-cemented in place. Under this "furry" hatband, glue a pair of small cotton eyebrows. Beneath the eyebrows, fasten two gummed stars. (Yes, this Santa will have stars in his eyes.) A Christmas seal or a small red circle will provide him with a nose. The flip-top lid is his mouth, so, around the opening, rubber-cement a cotton mustache and beard. If you wish, add a wispy fringe of cotton hair (on the side of the box and extending around the back). To attach the puppet to your tree, make a hole in the back of the box by press-

ing the point of a pencil through the cardboard. Then insert a firm (not droopy) branch of the tree.

To make his mouth move, hold Santa so that your thumb is at point *A,* the rest of your fingers at point *B* (see illustration). You'll find that gentle pressure of your hand will open and close his mouth.

This same little Santa can become a candy container for those cellophane-wrapped Christmas hard candies, at the party table or on the tree. Instead of standing the box on the table so that the flip-top lid is on the bottom, place it with the lid on top, and with the opening facing you. Make the hat as indicated above, but wrap the crepe paper around the lid itself. Now when you flip the lid to get the candy, Santa will tip his hat to you!

Rod Young's "Creative Marionette"

We were moving from New York to Los Angeles, and our last weekend was brightened by a farewell party given by the Puppetry Guild of Greater New York. Everyone performed, and when the president of the organization, Rod Young, sent his puppets on stage, they presented me with a gift. It was, as Rod's little "Fraidy Cat" puppet called it, a creative marionette. Won't you go creative with Fraidy Cat and me, and make yourself one, too? It's the simplest, most workable marionette I've ever seen.

You will need:

> The deep bottom half of a box (a shoe box would be fine)
> Strips of felt (3 thick, 2 thin, all about the same length)
> A crayon or felt-tipped pen
> Paints and brushes, or solid colored paper (if your box is covered with print or design)
> Approximately 1 1/2 yards of string
> Scissors
> Glue
> 2 empty flip-top cigarette boxes

Here's How: Place the bottom half of your box on a table so that the open part is facing down. If your box has printing or designs on it, paint it a light, solid color (or cover it with a solid colored paper). On one of the flat ends of the box, draw a big happy face (with crayon, pen, or paint). Glue the ends of two of the thick strips of felt to the top of the box, one on each side, so that they hang down near the face to form ears. Glue the end of the third thick felt strip to the top of the box, in the back, so that it droops down right in the center to form the tail.

Glue the ends of the two *thin* felt strips near the open bottom of the box, one on each side, and not too far from the face, so that they dangle down to form legs. Poke a small hole (with the point of a pencil or a pair of scissors) in the big, flat "hinged" back surface of one of the flip-top cigarette boxes. Into this hole insert the dangling end of the "leg" strip of felt, pull it through the hole and make a knot. This will keep the "leg" from becoming detached from the "foot" (the cigarette box). If your knot slips through the hole, enlarge the knot by making another one on top of the first.

In the same way, poke a small hole in the second cigarette box, and create the second "foot" on the other side, at the end of the other felt "leg."

On the top surface of your puppet (which was originally the bottom of your box), poke a tiny hole about two inches back from the face. Poke another tiny hole about $1^1/_2$ inches from the felt "tail."

Push one end of your piece of string into the hole near the face. (Insert it from above the box.) Now turn your box over so that the opening is facing up, and make a big knot in the end of the string that you've stuffed through the hole.

Turn your box over again (so that the opening is down) and slip the other end of the string (just the end, now) through the hole near the tail. Knot this end underneath, as you did the first. Flip the puppet over, lift him by his string "control," and there! You've done it! You've made a marionette with strings that can't possibly tangle — a miraculously maneuverable marionette. He has huge flat feet (the cigarette boxes) that beg you to bounce him a bit, or waddle him if you wish. I know you'll love him. No, no, no — don't thank me — thank Rod Young!

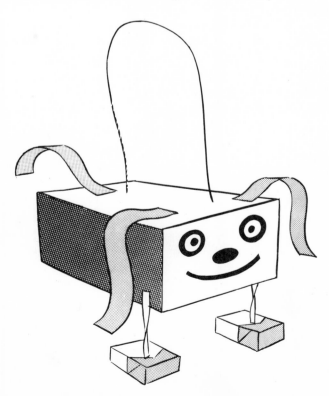

An Egg-citing Santa (although he's but a shell of his former self)

Eggzamine this puppet. Only an eggspert could tell what it is made of. Can you guess? Eggzactly!

You will need:
        A bowl
        A raw egg
        A needle
        Some cotton
        Rubber cement
        Construction paper or felt
        Scissors
        A handkerchief
        A rubber band

Here's How: With a large needle, prick a hole in each end of an egg. Holding it over a bowl, blow gently into the hole at one end and the insides of the egg will plop out of the shell through the hole at the other end. Enlarge just one of these holes gently, until your pointer finger can fit in. Apply rubber cement to the spot where you think Santa's beard should be, and then stick cotton right onto the rubber cement to form a big bushy beard. Do the same for the mustache, eyebrows, and hair. A tiny paper or felt cone will become his nose, and two other tiny pieces of paper or fabric his eyes. Make a larger cone of the same material (either paper or felt) for a hat, and trim it with cotton. Then rubber-cement the hat to the top of the egg. Now follow the instructions on page 65 and give Santa a drape body. Place Santa's head on top of the drape body and your puppet is ready to play.

Bouncer, the Ball Clown

This is the granddaddy of all easy puppets. I hope you have a ball with him!

You will need:
>A hollow or soft rubber ball
>Some cotton
>Rubber cement
>A party horn
>An old glove
>Some crayons or paint
>Scissors
>Paper or felt

Here's How: Cut a hole large enough for your pointer finger in a rubber ball. Crayon or paint a face on the ball and rubber-cement a neat frill of cotton around the finger hole. A party horn turned upside down is an ideal clown hat, or you can make a cone out of paper, color it, and rubber-cement it to the top of the ball. (If you prefer, make the cone out of felt.) Make a glove body (see page 67) and add little buttons of cotton (also rubber-cemented) to the palm of the glove. Place the ball clown head on the glove body, and he's ready to start clowning!

Hammond Public Library
Hammond, Ind.

The Talking Fish

You will need:

A rectangular piece of paper (half of a square)

Here's How: Bring the lower edge of the rectangle up to meet the upper edge. Crease sharply and open the paper.

1

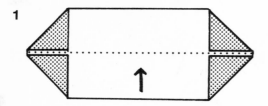

Fold each of the four corners to the center fold, so that your rectangle now comes to a sharp point at each side.

2

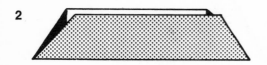

Fold the bottom edge of the oblong base up to meet the top edge. Do *not* sharpen this fold.

The center fold is now on the bottom.

3

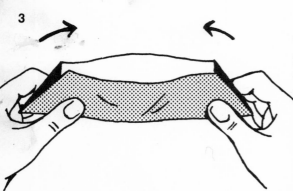

With one hand at each corner, grasp the paper along the center fold. Roll your hands upward and toward one another so that the center of the paper opens and the two points start to meet.

4

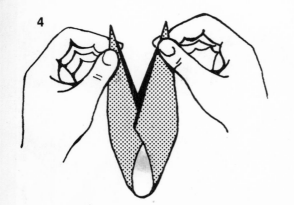

Slip the left point (and the two sides adjacent to the left point) into the right point.

Grip these points (now one within the other) in your right hand. This is the fish's mouth, so pinch firmly to keep it shut. Place your left pointer finger on the round section and tap gently toward the points until you have made a distinct indentation. Place the fish carefully on the table with your right pointer finger. Wipe your extended left pointer finger over the entire fish from tip to tail, flattening it. Sharpen the tail folds.

5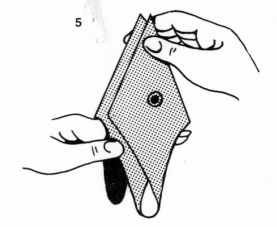

The tail is divided into two fins. Fold back the very tip of the upper fin. Turn the fish over, and fold the other fin the same way.

6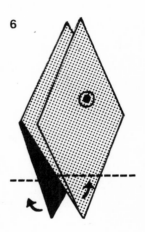

Grasp one of these tiny tail fins in each hand. When you pull your hands apart, the fish's mouth will open.

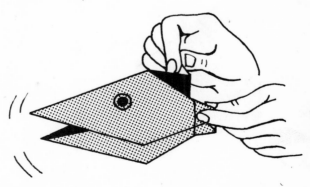

Billy Beak

You will need:
  A square piece of paper

Here's How: Bring the top point down to meet the bottom point, crease the paper sharply and open. Bring the two side points together, crease, and open it again.

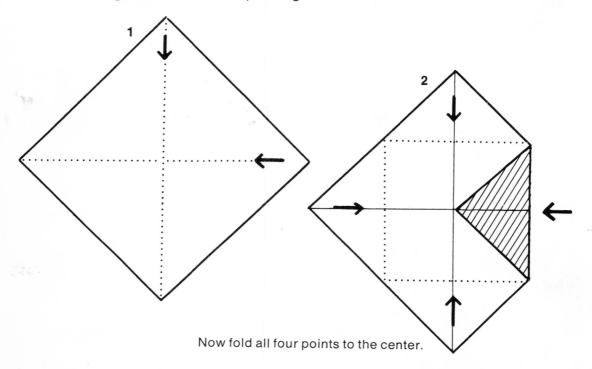

Now fold all four points to the center.

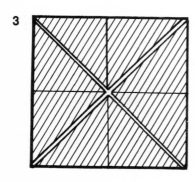

Turn the folded paper over.

Fold each of these new points to the center.

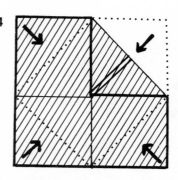

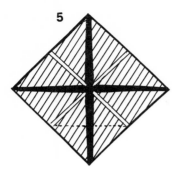

Fold the bottom point up to the mid-point of the square. Turn the paper over.

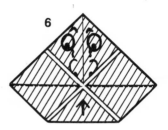

Fold the lower part of the figure up along the center crease . . . and slip it under the bottom part of the top point. This forms a little pocket under the point. Now is a good time to draw Billy's face.

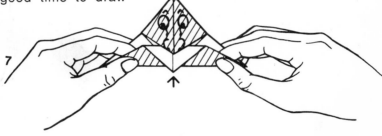

Fold the model back on itself through the center crease and open.

Press your hands gently together at the mid-point of the slanting sides and pull out the little pocket to form the lower part of Billy's beak. By moving your hands together and apart, Billy Beak will speak.

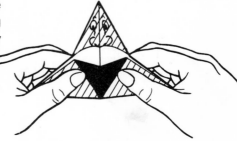

Sock Hobbyhorse Stick Puppet

The sock hobbyhorse can be made from that single sock your laundry was kind enough to return. If you're putting the hobbyhorse together for a single afternoon of play, cut the ears and eyes out of paper and paste them onto the sock, but if the hobbyhorse puppet is to be a permanent member of the family, cut the features out of leftover bits of fabric or felt and sew them in place. This little fellow will take about fifteen minutes to make, but he'll give you hours of pleasure, "horsin' around"!

You will need:

        A sock
        Clean ripped nylon stockings (for stuffing)
        A broom (a toy broom or a household broom)
        Bits of ribbon or heavy string
        Bits of felt, fabric, or paper
        Glue, paste, rubber cement, or pins, or needle and thread

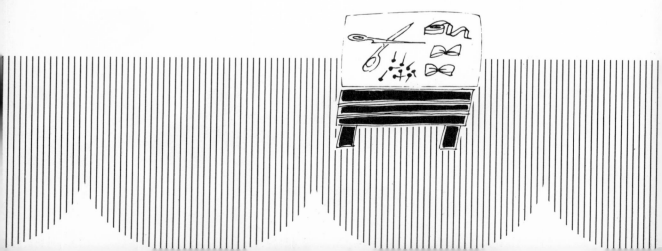

Here's How: Stuff the sock very full of discarded nylons. Insert the broom handle deep into the stuffed sock (twisting and turning it to get it through the stuffing, well into the sock). Tie the sock tightly around the broom handle with a piece of string or ribbon (see illustration). Cut round eyes, the size of quarters or half dollars, depending on the size of the sock, and triangular ears, out of felt, fabric, or paper. Glue or sew the eyes and ears in place. Tie the ribbon or string into eight to fifteen bows, and glue, pin, or sew them in a row down the back of the horse's head. That's his mane! Wrap one piece of ribbon or string around the front of his face — as if you wanted to keep his mouth shut!! Glue or sew it in position. Firmly attach the center of a much longer piece of ribbon or string to the place in front of his face, where his nose would be. Allow a long loop and then tie a knot. This is your hobbyhorse's reins. Hi-ho, Silver, away!

This puppet can be made with a large wooden cooking spoon as a base, or a dish mop, depending upon the size of the sock. He acts very well when worked from behind a chair, with a hand puppet riding on his back (that is, holding onto his stick). He can also perform within the cardboard stage (see page 71) and the doorway stage (see page 69).

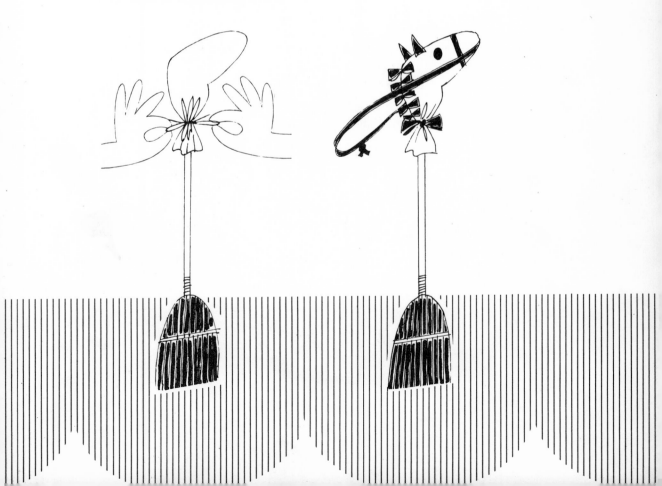

Spunky Monkey Glove Puppet

If you have a single unwanted glove (quite useless without its mate), you can turn it into a puppet that will be more fun than a barrel full of monkeys.

You will need:

> Tracing paper
> Scissors
> Light-colored felt or construction paper
> Soft pencil
> Any broken bits of jewelry (a single earring, a sequin, a
> > broken strand of beads, etc.)
> Glue or rubber cement
> A dark glove

Here's How: Place tracing paper over the hands, face, and tail patterns (see illustration) and trace the shapes and features. Cut out along the outlines, and transfer these shapes to the light-colored felt or construction paper. Cut out the felt or paper shapes. Draw the monkey's features on the felt or paper with a soft pencil.

Onto the monkey's head and hands, attach little bits of jewelry. Sew the drop part of pearl drop earrings to the monkey's ear or paste a fake diamond as an earring or attach a jeweled button. On his tiny fingers, try gluing sequin "rings." Now fasten the felt or paper face and hands to the glove. Place a dab of glue on the back of the little hand cutouts. Put the glove on your hand, and press the two felt or paper hands to the tips of your pointer and middle fingers. Dab a drop of glue onto the straight — not curled — end of the monkey's tail, and press it onto the glove, right above the back of your wrist. Now put glue on the reverse side of the monkey's face and fasten it, upside down, on the back of your hand. Turn your hand over and bend your wrist so that your fingers point down; hold your pinkie and ring fingers somewhat behind your pointer and middle fingers (on which you have pasted the monkey's hands). The tail, attached near your wrist, will perk up as you bend your wrist, and if you move your pointer and middle fingers, your little monkey will walk. He'll sit on your head, too.

Try making two monkeys on the same hand (see illustration). Simply attach one monkey hand to each of your finger tips, except your thumb, and put two tails at your wrist. Then paste two monkeys' heads on the back of your hand, right above the knuckles. Now sit back, move your fingers, and just watch all the monkeyshines!

If you have a spare mitten instead of a glove, you can make either Handy Andy (page 64), or Willie Talk (page 46), two easy mitten puppets.

Soap Sillies

These are very helpful puppets, for with their two little hands they can hold the soap, turn on the water, and even applaud you when you've done a good scrub-a-dub job!

You will need:
> Tracing paper
> Pencil
> Scissors
> A towel
> Straight pins
> Needle and thread
> Colorfast embroidery thread or bits of colored terry cloth from other old towels
> Small bits of colored toweling (optional)
> Colorfast binding tape (optional)

Here's How: Put a piece of tracing paper over page 45 and trace the puppet pattern. Enlarge the pattern one and one half inches all around. Cut out the enlarged outline. Fold the towel in half, pin the paper shape to the towel, trace the pattern, and then cut through the two layers of towel, along the outline. Sew the pieces together along the rounded edges, leaving only the flat bottom edge open. Turn the puppet inside out. On the round face, lightly pencil features. Embroider them with bright colorfast thread or cut them out of colored toweling and sew them in place. Ears (as on the bunny puppet in the illustration) or hat (as on the clown in the illustration) can be cut out of a colored towel, stuffed slightly with small bits of toweling, and sewn in place. Hem the bottom edge or bind with colorfast tape. Now put your pointer finger and your middle finger together into the head, your thumb into one arm, and your ring finger and pinkie into the other arm. This puppet can scratch his head or your back, so when you hop into the tub, the Soap Silly can do all the work. With him around, it won't be work, it'll be play.

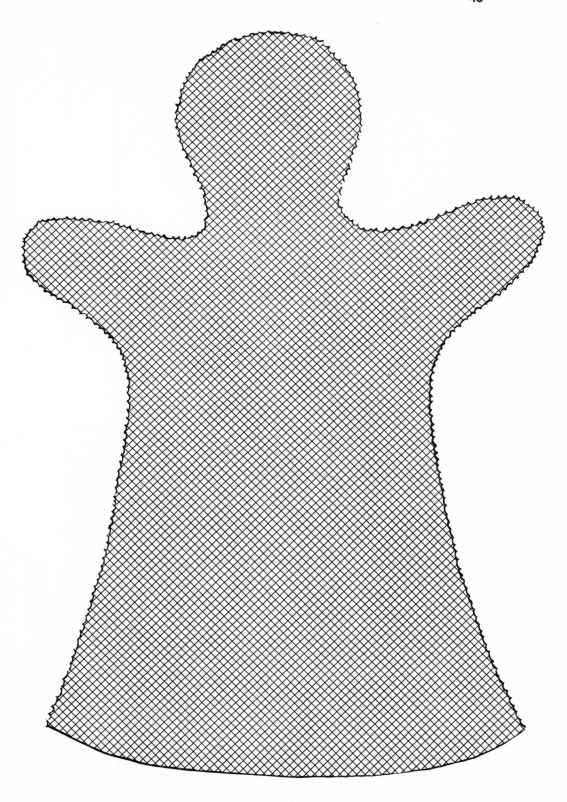

Willie Talk

This puppet is not only a helpful washcloth, he's good company.

You will need:
>Pencil
>Paper
>Scissors
>A towel
>Straight pins
>Needle and thread
>Colorfast embroidery thread or bits of colored terry cloth
>   from other old towels
>Colorfast binding tape (optional)

Here's How: Loosely trace the outline of your hand on a piece of paper. Keep all fingers together but your thumb. The outline will look just like a mitten. Enlarge the outline about a half inch all around, to allow for a seam. Then cut it out. Fold the towel in half, pin the paper pattern on the towel, and then cut along the outline through the two layers of towel. You now have two mitten shapes. Sew them together along the rounded edges, leaving the flat bottom part open. Turn the mitten inside out and put it on your hand. With a pencil, draw two eyes and a nose on the part of the mitten covering the back of your hand. The mouth is drawn at the point where the thumb meets the hand, with the top lip on the pointer finger, the lower lip on the thumb. Take off the mitten and either embroider the features with colorfast thread or cut them out of colored toweling and sew them in place. Hem the open edge or bind with colorfast binding tape. Put him on your hand, move your thumb up and down, and watch Willie Talk talk. If you slip a small cake of soap into the mitten and hold it in the palm of your hand, Willie Talk would be delighted personally to scrub your back!

Witch Hazel

Here's a bewitching witch.

You will need:

> One wooden spoon
> One party horn
> Some colored tape or construction paper
> Two paper reinforcements
> Sequins or gummed stars (optional)
> One cloth napkin or handkerchief
> One rubber band

Here's How: Hold the spoon with the hollow part facing you and the rounded part facing out. Stick the party horn right on top of the spoon to form the witch's hat. (If your horn has no fringe, stuff a few strands of wool or thin strips of paper under the horn so that your little witch will have straggly hair.) Now moisten the two paper reinforcements and stick them on the spoon to form big round eyes. If you wish, paste sequins, gummed stars, or tiny circles of colored paper inside the reinforcements' holes to make bright little eyeballs. Now cut from the tape or construction paper a long nose and a big mouth. My witch is a smiling sorceress, but yours can be the witch from Hansel and Gretel. Of course, she would then have a frown on her face.

Make the body (see page 65 for instructions). For fun, try pushing up the stick from the bottom (with the other hand, of course), and her neck will magically grow as long as a giraffe's. If you pull, her long neck will disappear.

Santa Plate Marionette

I discovered this little fellow during a Christmas party in the children's ward of a New York hospital. He's a decoration, he's a puppet, and he's a real doll!

You will need:

> 2 small paper plates (dessert size)
> 4 large paper plates (dinner size)
> A hole punch (optional)
> String
> Scissors
> Brass paper fasteners
> Red paint and brush
> Black construction paper
> Glue, paste, or rubber cement
> Cotton
> A ruler

Here's How: Hold the two small paper plates face to face with the bulges (bottoms) on the outside. At the top, punch a hole through the rims of the two paper plates and tie them together. Leave an extra length of string (for hanging). At the bottom, punch another hole through both plate rims. Now place the two large plates face to face and, in the same way, punch a hole at the top. Connect the top holes of the two large plates to the bottom holes of the two smaller ones, leaving about a half inch of slack string between them.

To make legs and arms, cut the rim off one of the two unused large plates and then cut the rim in half. At the bottom, insert these semicircular pieces between the two large plates to form legs. Fasten with paper fasteners. Cut the rim from the last unused large plate and trim this rim into shorter pieces, to serve as arms. Insert the arms between the two large plates (on the sides) and secure these with paper fasteners, too. Now paint the body (the large plates) and the arms and legs red. Dab just a bit of red paint on the very top of the small plates, to form the hat. Cut eyes, nose, and mouth out of black construction paper and paste them on the face (the small plates). Cut black paper gloves and boots.

When the paint has dried, glue the gloves and boots at the ends of the arms and legs. Attach (with glue) the cotton mustache, beard, buttons, belt, waist, and ankle cuffs, and the hat trim.

Enlarge all the holes around the paper fasteners so that the arms and legs can move easily. Make holes at the ends of his arms and legs and at the top of his head. Tie strings through these holes and attach them loosely to a ruler. Try hanging this Santa on your door, and see if your guests don't enter smiling!

Thumbelina

This little lady will always be right at your finger tips.

You will need:
>One thumb (preferably yours)
>A handkerchief
>A dark soft pencil, or a ball-point pen

Here's How: Draw Thumbelina's funny face on your thumb and dress her up in a big handkerchief by covering her head (be careful, not her face), and draping the handkerchief under her chin. You can vary this by drawing silly faces on peanut shells or thimbles and then putting them on your finger.

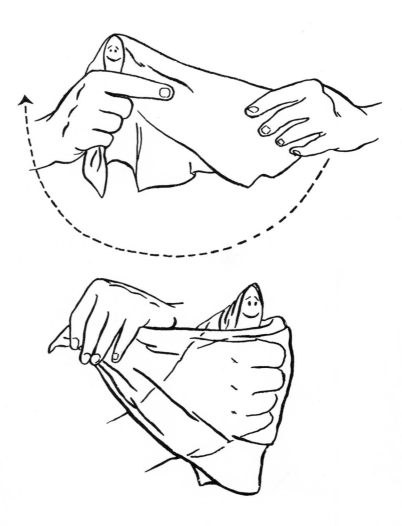

Hanky Panky

Any magician can pull a rabbit out of a hat, but can you pull a rabbit out of a handkerchief?

You will need:
> A handkerchief

Here's How: Make a loose wiggly fist with the fingers of your fist facing front, away from you. Drape a handkerchief over the entire fist. Now, with the other hand, grasp one of the corners of the handkerchief hanging in front of your fist (corner *B* in the diagram) and pull that corner up between the pointer finger and the middle finger of your fist. Hold the corner in place with those fingers as you do the same thing with the other corner hanging in front of the fist (corner *A* in the diagram). Bring it up and hold it in

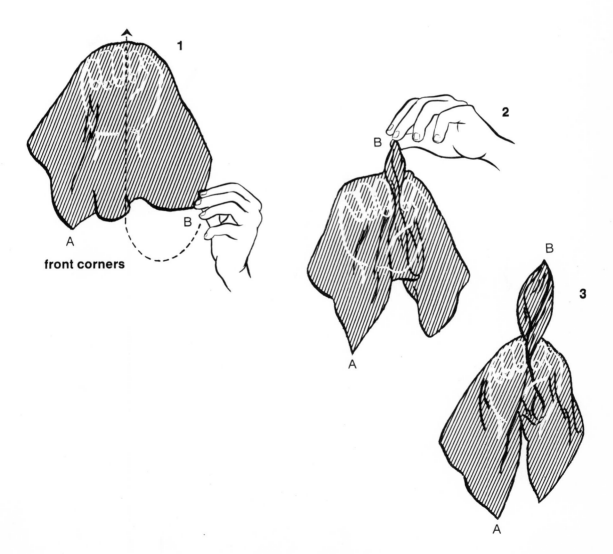

front corners

place between the middle and the ring finger of your fist. Your bunny now has two ears. Complete him by wrapping your wrists as firmly as you can. There.

By gently moving your fingers inside the handkerchief, you can make your bunny wiggle his nose and flap his ears. Perhaps he'll even nibble at a carrot and whisper in your ear.

Coppelia, the Dancing Handkerchief

Here's a dancing puppet who can kick and turn. You'll want to make her dance again and again. After all, one good turn deserves another.

You will need:
> A handkerchief

Here's How:　Make a knot in a handkerchief at point *A* along the edge and right in between two adjacent corners. Now hold the handkerchief upside down so that the knot is hanging as in the second picture. Holding those two corners firmly, twirl the handkerchief away from you, around and around, over and over again until all that remains is a twirled rope of hanky, with two loose ends and a knot in the center. Grasp the two twirled ends of the hanky rope in one hand and hold your hands as shown in picture 4. If you bring your hands together and apart slightly, the ballet

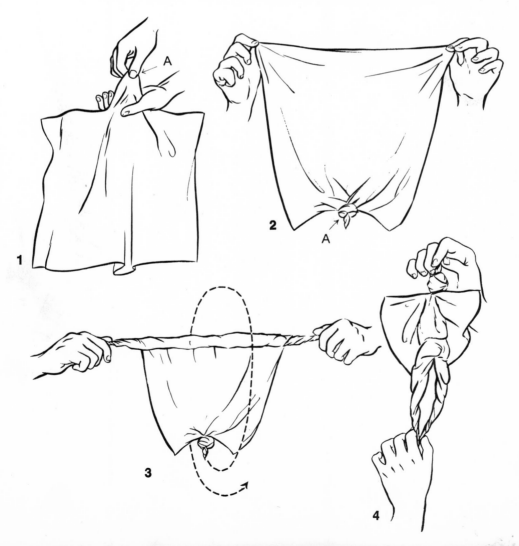

dancer will bend her knees and bow. To make her twirl and kick her legs high in the air, pull your hands rather sharply apart and let go of one leg. (But hold onto the other!) Wheeeeeeeee! You can make her go through her whirling dance over and over again by retwirling the hanky as in picture 3.

Winky

Winky is a handy little friend to have around.

You will need:
        Your hand (as clean as possible)
        A ball-point pen (or eyebrow pencil)

Here's How: Draw a face in the palm of your hand. Make sure that one eye straddles the fold in your palm directly under your pinkie. Hold your hand up next to your face and curl your fingers down halfway (see first picture). Now press down just your pinkie and quickly straighten it back to starting position (second picture). See how Winky will wink and flirt with you. See? You've got him in the palm of your hand!

Hand-some Johnny

Hand-some Johnny is a famous television star. Have you seen him?

You will need:
>A tube of dark lipstick
>Your hands

Here's How: With a lipstick, draw a face on the back of your hand. Follow the diagram for the position of the mouth. Carefully color the lower half of your pointer finger and the upper half of your thumb. But don't copy the features in the diagram. Draw any silly face that occurs to you. Now make a fist, wrapping the end of your pointer finger around the last joint of your thumb, so that your thumb becomes the lower lip, and your pointer finger becomes the upper lip. And that's all. As you move your thumb up and down, your puppet will talk, chew gum, eat, and sing.

Try sticking the thumb of your other hand through the mouth from inside the fist. Whoops! Looks like he stuck out his tongue at you, doesn't it? Tsk, tsk, tsk. Mustn't let this puppet get out of hand.

Starving Spaghetti Man

I'm a bit ashamed to say this sloppy eater makes me giggle every time I see him. I've constructed him on television and he evokes a flood of "do-it-again" mail.

You will need:
>A large sheet of paper
>Crayons
>Scissors or a sharp pencil
>A small ball of wool or string

Here's How: Starting at the top of the paper, draw a face with a round, round mouth. Below the face draw a napkin, tied around the neck. Add two hands, holding a fork and a knife. Then draw a straight line across the paper to indicate the edge of the table. On the table draw a plate, and lots and lots of wiggly lines on the plate. That's spaghetti! Make two holes (with a sharp pencil or the point of the scissors), one in the plate and the second in the Spaghetti Man's mouth. Now thread the loose end of the wool or string into the "plate" hole, entering the hole from the back of the picture and coming out in front. Extend the yarn in front of the picture up to the mouth hole (as in illustration) and insert the end of the wool into his open mouth. Pull it out in back. As you pull and pull and pull, your Starving Spaghetti Man will eat and eat and eat! I like best the moment when you get to the end of the wool and he slurps in the last strand of spaghetti.

Simple Sue

You will need:

A calling or business card or any small, rather stiff, paper rectangle

Pencil, crayon, or pen

Here's How: Draw two eyes and a nose near one end of the card. Bend, but do not fold, the rectangle in half with your left thumb on top, middle finger on the bottom, and your pointer finger sandwiched between the two layers. Place your right thumb and middle finger on opposite sides at the bend of the paper. Press the knuckle of your right pointer finger against this bend until you create a slight indentation.

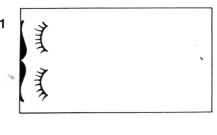

Now lift this right pointer finger and take away your left hand. Simply press your right thumb and middle finger together slightly and Simple Sue will speak for herself.

The Scissor Bird

This scissor bird is quite a cutup!

You will need:
        A sheet of construction paper (or other stiff paper)
        Crayons
        A blunt pair of scissors

Here's How: Draw a silly-looking bird, front or side view. Perhaps you'd like to add a real feather tail as I have. Next, draw two funny eyes, but instead of drawing the beak, stick the blades of a blunt pair of scissors through the paper at the spot where the beak should be. Now you can open or close your bird's beak by opening and closing the pair of scissors from behind the paper (which will cover your hand). If your bird becomes hungry, feed him scraps of paper and watch him chew them to pieces.

Just for fun, try making the same bird with a pair of pliers instead of scissors. Your bird will become a hook-beaked parrot. Spring clothespins, or Mother's hair clips form odd beaks, too.

Fly-by-Night, the Envelope Bird

This envelope bird is worth writing home about.

You will need:

        An envelope

        Crayon or postage stamp

Here's How: Place your hand into an envelope, with your fingers tucked into the corners, as in the first picture. At the arrow, press in with the fingers of the other hand. Now as you open and close your hand inside the envelope, your bird will open and close his beak. Complete your bird by adding an eye (in crayon, or by sticking on a postage stamp), and your talking envelope bird is sure to win the stamp of approval.

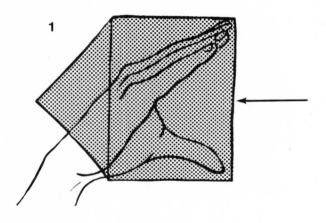

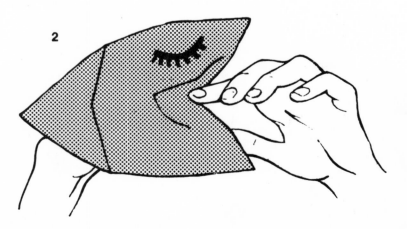

Mr. I. Glass, the Cup-pet

This paper-cup puppet, otherwise known as a "cup-pet," must live near water.

You will need:

> A paper cup with a handle
> A pencil

Here's How: Your paper cup should have a handle consisting of two circular flaps attached to the cup (and to each other) by a flat strip of cardboard. Open the two flaps until they look like a pair of eyeglasses. Draw two eyes inside the glasses and a round mouth under the connecting flat strip of cardboard. Push the pencil through the mouth circle, and, when you have made a hole, wriggle the pencil around to enlarge the mouth opening.

    You will find that if you hold Mr. I. Glass under a faucet, he will willingly drink the water (through the hole in the top of his head), but it will pour out of his mouth in the funniest way — I guess he's just not thirsty!

Bite-a-Bit, the Apple Puppet

One evening I invited my mother and father to dinner. After serving a giant-sized meal, I placed a bowl of fruit in the center of the table. Now any Arab worth his salt would have burped in order to show his appreciation of the feast that had been set before him. Not my father! He selected an apple and expressed his thanks by inventing a puppet for me on the spot. And what a puppet — moving mouth and all! You can make it, too, anywhere and anytime you have an apple handy.

You will need:
> A red apple
> Sharp teeth

Here's How: Hold an apple upside down. Find the widest, smoothest, shiniest, reddest surface, and take two tiny bites — not too far down and not too far apart. These are your puppet's eyes. Now nibble a nose. As you make the eyes and nose, bite away the skin so that the white flesh shows and glows brightly through the three little holes.

To make the moving mouth, turn the apple face upside down. Place your lower teeth at the point where you want your puppet's mouth to open. Spread your jaws until your upper teeth are resting on the flat top of the apple. Now bite UP, exerting most of the pressure with your lower teeth and as little as possible with your upper. When you've sunk your lower teeth up into the apple as far as you can, pull the apple up and away from your face (gently now!), gripping slightly with your lower teeth, leaving a strip of skin unbitten and unbroken at the top of this flap. You've given your puppet a moving mouth. Do you find that hard to swallow? Let me prove it to you. Cup the back of your puppet's head in the four fingers of your right hand and place your right thumb under the flap. By wiggling your thumb up and down, you'll make your puppet's mouth open and close. Try not to close it too firmly, because the juicy insides of his mouth will cause it to remain shut. If this happens, just shake the entire head, and his mouth will flop open again, waiting for you to put words into it.

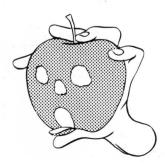

Your Gum Chum

Here's one fish that'll never clam up on you.

You will need:
>An empty cellophane-wrapped chewing gum box
>A needle
>Some thread

Here's How: Empty a box of Chiclets, for instance, or any other cellophane-wrapped box of gum, and push the transparent wrapping half off the box. Since you only pushed it half off, the other half is still around the box. Now grab the box, as shown in the diagram, holding both cellophane and box firmly in place. Thread a needle, knot the thread in a big fat knot, and insert the needle into the end of the cellophane and then through the end of the box itself. Push the needle and thread all the way through till the needle comes out the open end of the box and the knot is resting against the cellophane at the other end. Remove the needle, leaving the length of string. You will find that pulling gently on the string will cause the knot to press the center of the cellophane wrapping in toward the box, forming a funny fish mouth.

As you pull and release the pressure on your string, the fish will open and close his mouth. He'll nibble on noses and things that are offered to him, and if you care to give him a voice, he'll talk and talk and talk.

Handy Andy

For attaining that cleanliness that is next to godliness with the least unpleasantness, make and use Handy Andy.

You will need:
> Pencils
> Paper
> Scissors
> A towel
> Straight pins
> Needle and thread
> Colorfast embroidery thread or bits of colored terry cloth from other old towels
> Colorfast binding tape (optional)

Here's How: Loosely trace the outline of your hand on a piece of paper. Keep all your fingers together, so the outline looks like a mitten without a thumb. Enlarge the outline about a half inch all around, to allow for a seam. Then cut it out. Fold the towel in half and pin the paper pattern to the towel. Trace the pattern onto the towel and then cut along the outline through the double thickness of towel. You now have two thumbless-mitten shapes. Sew the pieces together along the rounded edges, leaving the bottom part open. Turn inside out and slip it on your hand. Pencil a simple face on the part of the mitten covering the palm of your hand. Make sure one eye straddles the fold in your palm directly under your pinkie. Take off the mitten and either embroider the features with colorfast thread, or cut them out of colored toweling and sew them in place. Hem the open bottom edge or bind it with the colorfast binding tape. At bathtime, slip him (or her) on (with the face over the palm of your hand), and when you bend your fingers down, he'll wink at you! He's not fresh — just friendly.

Puppet Bodies

Drape Body

This puppet body is as easy as 1-2-3 — fingers, that is.

You will need:

      A large handkerchief
      A rubber band

Here's How: Hold your hand with the last two fingers folded onto the palm and the other three extended as in the picture. Now drape a handkerchief evenly over the extended fingers. Hook a rubber band over the handkerchief around finger number 1 (your middle finger) and pull it back of your pointer finger (2) and hook it over the handkerchief and around your thumb (3). The head (a ball, or perhaps a fruit) is placed onto your pointer finger (2). The thumb and middle finger (1 and 3) become your new friend's hands — and there he is, right at your finger tips, ready to do your bidding.

Ella Fant, the elephant puppet with the turnip head (see page 25) has a cotton handkerchief body like the one described above.

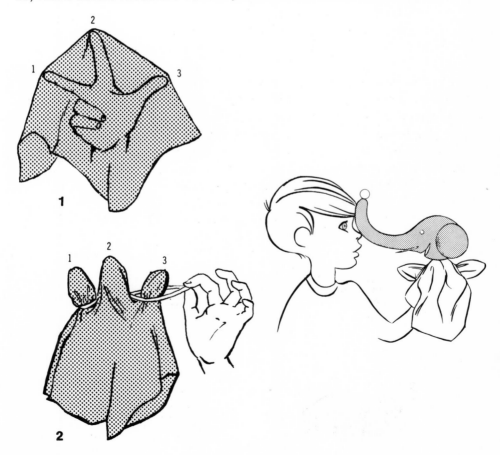

Drape-Around-Stick Body

If you want a puppet friend with real backbone, try one built around a stick of some sort. You can use a wooden spoon, or perhaps a carrot.

You will need:

A stick
A rubber band
A handkerchief

Here's How: Wrap the last three fingers of your right hand around the stick, with your pointer finger and thumb extending in opposite directions. Drape the handkerchief or cloth over the two extended fingers, and hook a rubber band around the pointer finger, then in back of the stick, and last, around the thumb. Make a face on the part of the stick that extends above your hand, and there he is — a little fellow that nobody will ever call spineless.

Witch Hazel (page 47) and Captain Carrot (page 23) have bodies made in this way.

Glove Body

Next time you lose one glove, drop the remaining one in your rainy day box, for you will find that a glove body will complete your ball, matchbox, or fruit puppet very well indeed.

You will need:
> One old glove
> Scissors

Here's How: Cut off the ring finger and the pointer finger of the glove, leaving just enough fabric to tuck in (for neatness' sake). If you are working with a left glove, put it on your right hand, or vice versa. Hold your right hand as in the diagram, with the last two fingers folded onto the palm. Now stick *your* right thumb into the thumb of the left glove, your right pointer finger into the middle finger of the left glove, and your right middle finger into the pinkie of the left glove.

Actually, if you'll just insert your right-hand finger number 1 into the number one left glove, then your right number 2 finger into the number two left glove finger, etc., it will come out right. Your pointer finger (number 2) is the one that goes into the hole in your puppet head, and the thumb and middle finger become the arms. Now move your fingers and see how he comes to life for you!

Bouncer, the Ball Clown (page 35), has a body like this.

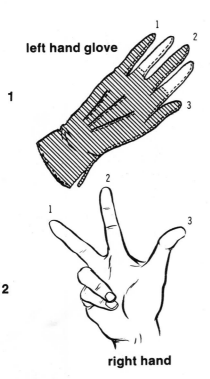

left hand glove

right hand

Puppet Stages

Apron Stage

This stage is most fun when three or more friends are playing together.

You will need:
> A big colorful apron

Here's How: The girl in the center ties an apron around her waist. Her two friends stand one on each side of her. The girl wearing the apron has two puppets, one on each hand. Each of her friends has one puppet. They are wearing their puppets on the hand closest to the girl with the apron. At a given signal, they reach down with their outside hands (that is, the hand farthest *away* from the girl with the apron), and, grabbing the bottom corner of the apron that is closest to them, they lift it way above their heads. The apron (if it's the right size) will cover the girl in the middle completely. She can lift up both of her hands so that her puppets are dancing right above the bottom hem of the apron. The two children who are apron holders can hold up their puppets behind the apron, too, so that all four puppets can perform at the same time.

Doorway Stage

If Mother will lend you a sheet or a blanket, you can make a doorway stage.

You will need:
> A sheet or blanket
> Thumbtacks

Here's How: Attach your sheet or blanket across an open doorway at a point about one inch above your head. You will find that when you stretch your arms up, your hands will show over the sheet or blanket, but you will be completely hidden. Place two of your favorite puppets on your hands and let them peek out above the sheet, and sing and dance along the top rim. It might be fun at a party to let children take turns having their puppets lead the group in community singing and games of Follow the Leader and Simon Says.

Tray Stage

This is a very unusual stage and easy to make.

You will need:

The shallow top cover of a cardboard box
Scissors
Some paint
Some ribbon or heavy string

Here's How: Cut two holes, large enough for your hand to fit through, in the top of the box. Paint the entire box top a gay color. Attach a long piece of ribbon or string to each of the four corners of the box top and tie the four loose ends around your neck so that the cover hangs parallel to the floor. Now put your hands up through the holes, put the puppets on your hands, and let them play, right there, on top of their own tiny stage. You can carry this stage with you wherever you go.

Cardboard Carton Stage

This puppet stage takes a bit more time to construct, but it is, nevertheless, easy enough for anyone to build.

You will need:

A large carton
Paints or crayons
Scissors
A bridge table
A sheet or blanket

Here's How: Select a large sturdy grocery carton and decide which side is going to be the front and which the back. Remove the back of the carton entirely and cut the front so that you get the effect of a curtain drape (follow dotted lines in diagram). Next paint the entire box a bright color. Cover a bridge table with a sheet or blanket and place your cardboard carton stage on top of the table. Place the back edge of the carton right along the back edge of the table.

If you kneel behind the table, the blanket or sheet on the table will hide you, but the puppets on your hands can perform in the opening of the cardboard carton stage. If you want to change puppets in the middle of your play, line up the other puppets on the floor under the table, and no one will see them because of the drape.

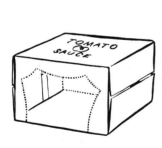

Puppets and Things to Do with Them

How to Make Friends with a Puppet

Some of my best friends are puppets. . . .

Any doll-like toy that moves or "animates" is accurately called a puppet. A string puppet is called a marionette, while a hand puppet is one in which your hand is inside the figure. (Generally, your pointer finger goes into the neck or head, while your thumb becomes one arm, and your middle finger the other.)

I like hand puppets best because they come to life with so little effort. Is your little puppet puzzled about something? Rub your thumb against the side of your pointer finger and see him scratch his head. Is your puppet happy? Simply bring your thumb and middle finger together, and I'll bet he'll clap his hands. Is he hungry? Make him rub his tummy. Is he frightened? He can cover his eyes.

You'll discover many lively, funny things for your puppet to do. There are no rules. I would suggest that you try not to jiggle your character — fewer, broader gestures will be less confusing. When you have more than one puppet at a time on stage, it's advisable that you move only the one that is supposed to be talking.

Sit in front of a mirror for a few minutes with your puppet on your hand and watch him — he'll show you how best to make him move.

Help your puppets to travel right onto and off the stage. Let them ride on cars, planes, boats, or horses. These can be very light toys that have rulers or long pencils taped or pasted to them (or stuck into them), or cutouts of magazine pictures that have been pasted to cardboard, with sticks attached behind them (see pages 82-83 for instructions).

Rainy Day Box

The hardest part of any play project is the assembling of materials. Why not start a "Rainy Day Box" — a scrap box full of this and that, bits and pieces, things you have stowed away instead of thrown away. Then on that "nothing-to-do day" that rolls 'round every so often, you'll be fully prepared.

Here's a list of odds 'n' ends that will come in handy in making simple puppets.

Torn gloves and mittens
Old socks
Clean torn nylon stockings
Balls that have lost their bounce
Discarded jewelry
Old nice magazine pictures
Old hats (all kinds)
Construction paper
Scissors
Big, clean, but frayed handker-
    chiefs
Balloons
Scraps of material
Bits of fur
Brown wrapping paper
Small paper bags
Old pocketbooks
String
Cellophane
Paper doilies
Crayons
Tiny buttons
Empty gift boxes and lids for
    stages
Thumbtacks
Feathers
Glue and rubber cement
Scotch tape
Pipe cleaners
Pieces of old lace
Colored gift wrapping paper
Leftover strands of wool
Crepe paper
Cotton batting
Rubber bands
Party horns and hats

Fiddle the Riddle

It might be fun to have a special puppet character who could be a riddle master. (I have found that most boys and girls enjoy the challenge of a good riddle.)

Your riddle master could try to stump your family or friends with riddles like these:

Why does an Indian wear a feather headdress?
   — To keep his wig wam.

Which is the strongest day of the week?
   — Sunday. The rest are weak days.

What is it that a cat has that no other animal has?
   — Kittens.

What is yours, but used by others more than you use it?
   —Your name.

What fish's eyes are nearest together?
   — The smallest fish.

Why do hurricanes always have a girl's name?
   — Because they're *her*-icanes, not *him*-icanes.

Storytime

Stories are exciting beginnings for puppet plays. Those stories that you know, and that all your friends know too, can simply be improvised. Each child, having made or been given the right puppet character has his puppet say and do whatever he thinks the character in the story would be saying and doing at that moment. Stories in this category include:

"Three Little Pigs"
"Goldilocks"
"Little Red Riding Hood"
"The Little Red Hen"
"The Gingerbread Boy"

Many of the well-known Bible stories (such as Moses in the Bulrushes, Joseph and His Brothers, David and Goliath, Noah and the Ark) lend themselves to this treatment.

There are so many *more* enticing tales, though, that it would seem a pity to limit your puppet plays to those you know. Why not have someone read a new story as you, with the appropriate puppets, act it out in pantomime? Try these. They're wonderful!

For Halloween — Witch tales like "The Salad" (Grimm), or "Rapunzel"

For Thanksgiving — Feast tales like "Three Wishes" or "Why the Sea Is Salt"

For Christmas — Happy generous tales like "The Shoemaker and the Elves"

For Easter — Bunny tails (ooops — I mean tales) like "The Whiskers of Ho Ho" (Littlefield)

For St. Patrick's Day — Irish folk tales like "Little Dermot and the Thirsty Stones"

For April Fools' Day — Puckish tales like "The Merry Pranks of Tyll Eulenspiegel"

For Any Wonderful Day — Curious tales like the *Just So Stories* (Kipling)

All of these stories can be found in the library, and make good reading whether you "play" them or not.

Don't try to write a script, or learn your part — just pick a story you love, and everyone else will love it, too!

Sing Along

It's amazing how well puppets sing, considering what they're made of. . . .

Some songs are fun to act out with puppets ("Ten Li'l Indians" and "Old MacDonald" lend themselves beautifully to this kind of dramatization). Other song games are nice to *play* with puppets: "The Farmer in the Dell," "She'll Be Comin' Round the Mountain," and "Here We Go Round the Mulberry Bush," to name a few.

Try three puppets, conducting three groups of your friends in rounds. ("The King of France," and "Row Row Row Your Boat," or "Three Blind Mice," for example — but not at the same time, please!)

Puppets, I have found, play musical instruments very well indeed. (As well as you can play them, I'll bet!) They have particular skill with drums, cymbals, wood blocks, tuned bells, xylophones, tiny pianos, and other toy instruments they can shake, rattle, or bang. Try it, and you'll see that you and your puppet can make beautiful music together.

Puppets and Very Small People

(Additional Advice on Puppetry for the Preschool, Nursery School, and Early Grades Child, from the Mother of a Five-Year-Old Girl.)

Forgive me if I remove my puppeteer's hat and speak now as "Mallory's Mother." I've revised many of my beliefs about puppets and little people in the past year, for my daughter Mallory and her many friends (in school and in our home) have taught me what I can and cannot expect them to do. May I suggest:

1. It is not a good idea for too many children to make these puppets together — usually three or four is the number any one adult can handle happily at one time.

2. Let the children use the material freely and help them to use it as the need arises, rather than trying to teach them techniques before they are given the material with which to work. In this way children will be able to fulfill their needs of the particular moment more joyously. Don't try to use the puppets the children have just made to do a puppet play, or for any kind of performance by the children, or even for display purposes. They may very well spontaneously and informally enjoy acting out something, but I believe that young children should not be expected or encouraged to give performances using their own puppets.

3. Don't feel that it is absolutely necessary for small children to make their own puppets from scratch. Stick puppets made from cutouts or from small stuffed toys may be more feasible. I've always found that papier-mâché heads were too heavy for children. Their hands got tired and they discarded the entire project before long. Cardboard tubes from toilet paper rolls, cut in half (or thirds, or even quarters for tiny hands) are easy to decorate with those little gummed stars that can be bought in the 5 & 10, and which create wonderful and immediately recognizable faces.

Here's the general recipe for stick puppets:

Cut pictures out of magazines — good-sized pictures of people, animals, and objects that you'd like to have as props and scenery (cars, airplanes, houses, machinery, and trees, are very useful). Keep these in a separate box until you have a good collection of pictures of both grownups and children. Then make your stick puppets.

Cut each figure out very carefully and paste it on top of a piece of shirt cardboard. Then cut the entire figure out of the cardboard. Tape or glue a big pencil or a ruler or a thick strip of heavy cardboard to the back of your cutout figure. When you have one puppet for each character in the story you want to tell, the child can kneel behind an armchair so that the people who are watching can see the puppets but can't see the puppeteer. Have the child hold the puppet up in the air so that the bottom of the puppet "walks" or "sits" right on top of the chair so that very little of the stick shows. Let the stick puppet actors "ride" in stick puppet boats, or cars (also pasted to rulers or rods).

These stick puppets are very delightful when used inside the cardboard carton stage, too (see page 71 for instructions).

Another excellent basic form of stick puppet can be instantly created with old stuffed toys and rulers (or small rods or sticks of wood). Make a little hole in the bottom of the stuffed animal, insert the stick, and sew the hole closed around the stick. These dimensional stick puppets can be worked from behind chairs and sofas, or from behind the doorway stage (see page 69) or the cardboard carton stage (see page 71).

Experiment with the toilet paper roll puppet, too. Slice a toilet paper roll in thirds or in quarters, depending on the size of the small puppeteer's pointer finger. Either paste pretty paper around your roll, paint it, color it with crayons, or cover with skin-color crepe paper. Add features either by pasting on gummed stars, by gluing on features cut out of paper, or by drawing or painting them. This roll sits on the pointer finger. If you want to make a body for the roll puppet, try the drape body (page 65).

To add hair to the toilet paper roll puppet, fringe a piece of paper and paste it to the sides and on top of the puppet's head. Little bits of fur pasted around the rim, or a few lengths of wool cut to the right size, knotted together in the middle and draped down the sides would also be lovely.

Puppet Aids for the Teacher and Group Leader, and a Holiday Index

Most of the puppets in the first section (Puppets for Plays) can be adapted to create any traditional holiday figure. For example, Willie B. Brave, the Matchbox Indian, could be Santa Claus, or a clown, or a Valentine sweetheart (with a construction-paper heart pasted on for a face). He could become George Washington himself, with a magazine picture of Mr. Washington's face cut out and pasted to the front of the box.

A paper bag turned upside down and manipulated as we have in the case of Sad Sack, the Bunny, can serve as the base for any talking character required — as long as the mouth of the figure is drawn right at the bottom fold.

The egg puppet (Egg-citing Santa) and the ball puppet (Bouncer, the Ball Clown) are examples of versatile form, too, and its potential is limited only by the contents of your Rainy Day Box.

The spoon stick puppet (Witch Hazel) is a convertible puppet concept (how about a giraffe with a neck that stretches?), and of course, the Soap Sillies puppet, made of regular fabric (instead of a terry towel) and decorated accordingly, can be used to fill almost any of your theatrical needs.

When you explore the realm of fruit puppets, the possibilities are tremendous. Captain Carrot, Ella Fant (the turnip puppet), and Apple Jack 'n' Jill are three starting points — but try *carving* the puppet head out of an apple, and then watch your character age right before your eyes as the apple shrivels and browns.

Potato heads are utilitarian, too, and can be decorated according to your own needs.

Pears with their "round jowls" make fine faces.

Experiment with flip-top cigarette packs (the kind that have hinged flaps at the top). This flap, placed at the bottom, makes a superb moving mouth (as in Smokey the Santa).

A number of the puppets described in this book are directly applicable for holiday use.

For Easter, see The Funny Bunny (page 16), Sad Sack, the Bunny (page 19), and Hanky Panky (page 51).

For Halloween try Boo Hoo, the Little Ghost (page 18), Apple Jack 'n' Jill (page 27), and Witch Hazel (page 47).

For Columbus Day see Captain Carrot (page 23), and Willie B. Brave, the Matchbox Indian (page 28).

At Christmas time make Smokey the Santa (page 30), Egg-citing Santa (page 34), and the Santa Plate Marionette (page 48).

You might enjoy decorating your entire Christmas tree with homemade puppets, too.

Jack-in-the-Bag (page 21), Willie B. Brave (page 28), Smokey the Santa (page 30), and Santa Plate Marionette (page 48) would love to hang around your tree.

Hammond Public Library
Hammond, Ind.

Puppet Books — A Bibliography

Art of the Puppet
    Bill Baird (New York: The Macmillan Company, 1965)
Chinese Puppet Theater
    Sergei V. Obraztsov (Boston: Plays, Inc., 1961)
Dolls and Puppets
    Max von Boehn (New York: Cooper Square Publishers, Inc., 1967)
Expert Puppet Technique
    Eric Bramall and C. C. Somerville (Boston: Plays, Inc., 1963)
Folding Paper Masks
    Shari Lewis and Lillian Oppenheimer (New York: E. P. Dutton & Co., Inc., 1965)
Folding Paper Puppets
    Shari Lewis and Lillian Oppenheimer (New York: Stein & Day, 1962)
Folk Plays for Puppets You Can Make
    Tom H. Tichenor (Nashville: Abingdon Press, 1959)
Handbook of Fist Puppets
    Bessie Ficklen (New York: J. B. Lippincott Co., 1935)
History of English Puppet Theater
    Speaight (Boston: Plays, Inc., 1963)
Let's Look At Puppets
    A. R. Philpott (London: Frederick Muller)
Practical Puppetry
    John Mulholland (New York: Arco Publishing Company, Inc., 1962)
Punch and Judy
    Ed Emberly (New York: Little, Brown and Company, 1965)
The Puppet Book
    White, Wall, Philpott (Boston: Plays, Inc., 1966)
The Puppet Theater Handbook
    Marjorie Batchelder (New York: Harper & Row, Publishers, 1947)
The Puppet Theater of the Modern World
    Margaret Niculescu (Boston: Plays, Inc., 1967)
Puppets and Plays
    Marjorie Batchelder and Virginia Comer (New York: Harper & Row, Publishers, 1956)
Puppets and Puppetry
    Cyril Beaumont (London: Studio Publications, 1958)